Fact Finders®

ADVENTURES ON THE AMERICAN FRONTIER

CUTTING A PATH

DANIEL BOONE AND THE CUMBERLAND GAP

BY ELIZABETH RAUM

Consultant:
Robert Morgan
Kappa Alpha Professor of English
Cornell University

CAPSTONE PRESS
a capstone imprint

Fact Finders are published by Capstone Press,
1710 Roe Crest Drive, North Mankato, Minnesota 56003
www.capstonepub.com

LIBRARY OF CONGRESS CATALOGING-IN-PUBLICATION DATA
Raum, Elizabeth.
  Cutting a Path: Daniel Boone and the Cumberland Gap/by Elizabeth Raum.
    pages cm.—(Fact finders: Adventures on the American frontier)
  Summary: "Examines the Wilderness Trail (i.e., the Cumberland Gap) by discussing how and why it came to be and the immediate and lasting effects it had on the nation and the people who traveled it"—Provided by publisher.
  Audience: Grades 4–6.
  Includes bibliographical references and index.
  ISBN 978-1-4914-4895-3 (library binding); ISBN 978-1-4914-4909-7 (paperback);
  ISBN 978-1-4914-4927-1 (ebook PDF)
1. Wilderness Road—Juvenile literature. 2. Frontier and pioneer life—Tennessee, East—Juvenile literature. 3. Frontier and pioneer life—Kentucky—Juvenile literature. 4. Frontier and pioneer life—Virginia—Juvenile literature. 5. Boone, Daniel, 1734–1820—Juvenile literature. 6. United States—Territorial expansion—Juvenile literature. I. Title.
  F454.R38 2015
  976.902092--dc23   2015007848

EDITORIAL CREDITS
Jennifer Huston, editor; Kazuko Collins, designer;
Tracy Cummins, media researcher; Laura Manthe, production specialist

PHOTO CREDITS
Alamy: Jim Lane, 13; Bridgeman Images: Look and Learn/Severino Baraldi, 11, 23; Corbis: GraphicaArtis, 4; CriaImages.com: Jay Robert Nash Collection, Cover; Flickr: Internet Archive Book Images, 14; Getty Images: Kean Collection/Archive Photos, 21, Photo Researchers, 9; Granger, NYC: 6, 26; Newscom: Picture History, 18; North Wind Picture Archives: 24; Shutterstock: Itana, Design Element, ixer, Design Element, Miloje, Design Element, Picsfive, Design Element; Wikimedia: National Atlas of the United States, 7, Nikater, 17.

PRIMARY SOURCE BIBLIOGRAPHY
Page 4, Line 13: John Mack Faragher. *Daniel Boone: The Life and Legend of an American Pioneer.*
        New York: Henry Holt and Company, 1992, p. 114.
Page 5, callout quote: Felix Walker. "The First Settlement of Kentucky: Narrative of an Adventure in
        Kentucky in the Year 1775." *DeBow's Review, Vol. 16.* February 1854, p. 152.
Page 11, caption: Michael A. Lofaro. *Daniel Boone: An American Life.* Lexington: The University Press
        of Kentucky, 2003. p. 18.
Page 11, callout quote: John Filson. *The Discovery, Settlement, and Present State of Kentucke.*
        Westminster, Md.: Heritage Books, Inc., 1996, p. 56.
Page 19, callout quote: *DeBow's Review, Vol. 16.* p. 154.
Page 22, callout quote: *The Discovery, Settlement, and Present State of Kentucke.* p. 65.
Page 25, callout quote: Ellen Eslinger, ed. *Running Mad for Kentucky: Frontier Travel Accounts.*
        Lexington: University Press of Kentucky, 2004, p. 36.
Page 28, Line 2: *Daniel Boone: An American Life.* p. 152.

Printed in Canada.
052015   008825FRF15

TABLE OF CONTENTS

———— • ◆ • ————

A JOURNEY THROUGH THE WILDERNESS

In March 1775, Daniel Boone and his crew left their homes to cut a road through the Cumberland Gap to Kentucky. For 200 miles (322 kilometers), they labored up and down rugged mountains, through dense forests and murky swamps, and across rivers and streams. An early traveler described the road as "hilly, stony, slippery, [and] bushy." But it led to Kentucky, and that was their goal.

Daniel Boone owned a farm, but he preferred hunting and trapping in the forest.

The ax blades hacked away as the men chopped down trees large and small. For several hours each day, they burned dead brush and cut through thick patches

> "A new sky and strange earth seemed to be presented to our view. So rich a soil we had never seen before; covered with clover in full bloom, the woods were abounding with wild game—turkies so numerous that it might be said they appeared but one flock ..."
>
> —Diary entry of Felix Walker, who helped cut the Wilderness Road

of **cane** and reeds. After nearly two weeks of backbreaking work, they arrived at a land with rich soil, fields of clover, and woods full of **game**. They had passed through the Cumberland Gap and had reached the fabled land of Kentucky.

Even so, Boone and his crew were still 15 miles (24 km) away from their final **destination**. They spent the night of March 24 on the banks of Silver Creek near present-day Milford, Kentucky. But by dawn, two of Boone's men would be dead.

The Cumberland Gap

Located near where the states of Kentucky, Tennessee, and Virginia meet, the Cumberland Gap is a narrow break in the Cumberland Mountains. The Cumberlands are part of the Appalachian Mountain Range. The Appalachians stretch 1,500 miles (2,414 km) from southeastern Canada to central Alabama. They formed a natural barrier between the original 13 colonies and the lands to the west. For years, American Indians and herds of migrating elk and buffalo crossed the mountains through the Cumberland Gap. In the late 1600s, European explorers and traders began using it too.

In Colonial times, the Cumberland Gap served as a gateway to the West.

Early Explorers

Historians believe that the first European to travel through the Cumberland Gap may have been an **indentured servant** named Gabriel Arthur. In 1673 he explored areas of present-day Tennessee. Eventually traders from Virginia, Pennsylvania, and the Carolinas made their way through the Gap. They **bartered** with the Indians, trading cloth, guns, and ammunition for animal furs. These traders described a beautiful country where game was plentiful, especially around the many natural salt licks. Their tales excited hunters like Daniel Boone, who dreamed of hunting in the land beyond the Gap.

Preserving a Way of Life

In the late 1700s there were no permanent Indian settlements in what is now Kentucky. However, members from at least a dozen tribes traveled in and out of the area to hunt. Large herds of elk, buffalo, and deer roamed the forests. So did bears, wolves, and wildcats, as well as smaller game such as turkeys, geese, and squirrels. Carp, catfish, sturgeon, and perch filled the rivers, and thousands of birds flew overhead.

The Indians depended on the wildlife for survival. They feared that the white settlers would claim the land for themselves. Loss of their hunting grounds would force the Indian families to move elsewhere in search of food. To protect their land, American Indians attacked men who were using the trail.

NORTH AMERICA IN 1775

HUDSON BAY COMPANY
49°
NOVA SCOTIA
MAINE (PART OF MASSACHUSETTS)
CLAIMED BY NEW YORK AND NEW HAMPSHIRE
NEW HAMPSHIRE
MASSACHUSETTS
NEW YORK
RHODE ISLAND
CONNECTICUT
PROVINCE OF QUEBEC
PENNSYLVANIA
WHITE SETTLEMENT BOUNDARY
NEW JERSEY
DELAWARE
VIRGINIA
MARYLAND
PROPERTY OF SPAIN
NORTH CAROLINA
INDIAN RESERVE
SOUTH CAROLINA
GEORGIA
WEST FLORIDA
EAST FLORIDA

KEY
- Britain's 13 American Colonies
- Other British Territory
- Spanish Territory

WHAT'S A LICK?

A "lick" is a spring that contains deposits of minerals such as calcium, sodium, and iron. Animals need these minerals for bone and muscle growth, so they often gather to lick the mineral salts or deposits.

The licks were important for settlers too. Salt not only adds flavor to food, it also preserves meat.

CHAPTER 2

DANIEL BOONE: HUNTER AND TRAILBLAZER

Daniel Boone was born in Pennsylvania on November 2, 1734. When he was 13, his father gave him a hunting rifle. Boone quickly became an excellent **marksman**. As he roamed the woods, he met other hunters, both white and American Indian. They taught him a common language that included English, French, and Dutch words. He was at home in the forest and considered the Indians his friends.

When Daniel was 16, the Boone family moved to the Yadkin Valley of North Carolina. It was there that Daniel met and married Rebecca Bryan in 1756. Over the years, they had 10 children.

As an adult, Boone was strong, quick, and calm in emergencies. He owned a farm, but Rebecca did most of the farming. Boone made more money hunting and then selling the animal skins and furs he collected.

FUN FACT

In the mid-1700s, an average deerskin was worth about $1 at market. A buck is a male deer, so hunters like Boone began to call a dollar "one buck."

Daniel Boone and his men get their first glimpse of Kentucky.

Blazing a Trail

During the winter of 1768–1769, trader John Findley visited the Boones. Findley needed a guide to help him find the gap in the Cumberland Mountains that led to Kentucky. Boone did not hesitate. He gathered a small band of hunters, and they left with Findley on May 1, 1769.

Boone led the group along the Yadkin River, over several mountains, and into Powell's Valley on the western edge of what is now Virginia. From there they followed a hunter's trail called the Warrior's Path through the Cumberland Gap. From a high ridge called Pilot's Knob, Boone saw Kentucky for the first time.

LONG HUNTERS

Boone was one of Kentucky's long hunters. From October until March or later, these men left their families to hunt in the wilderness. They often started in large groups of 50 or 60 men and then broke into smaller groups of two or three. These long hunters faced rough living conditions, bad weather, hunting accidents, and Indian attacks. Even so, they preferred hunting to farming and the wilderness to settled towns.

Exploring Kentucky

Findley followed the Warrior's Path north to a Shawnee trading post near present-day Winchester, Kentucky. The others went into central Kentucky for better hunting.

For the next two years, Boone explored Kentucky, traveling as far as present-day Louisville. He was amazed by the dense forests, animals of all kinds, fields of wild clover, and fresh waters filled with fish. He made Indian-style camps, found shelter in caves, or slept in his canoe.

Alone in the wilderness and far from help, Boone faced fierce bears and hungry wolves. A simple accident could mean death. So could a run-in with any of several American Indian tribes who were at war with each other. The Iroquois were fighting the Cherokee and Catawba. The Shawnee and Delaware were fighting the Cherokee. Boone avoided them whenever possible. Even so, both Indians and wolves raided his camps and made off with valuable furs and supplies.

Although Daniel Boone is often shown in paintings wearing a coonskin cap, he never wore one.

When Boone finally returned home in May 1771, he couldn't stop thinking about Kentucky. He soon began planning a move to the land of his dreams. But he wasn't the only one planning to move there. Interest in the area was growing as other hunters and traders made their way to Kentucky. Boone needed to act quickly before others claimed the best land.

"I was happy in the midst of dangers ... No ... city ... could afford so much pleasure to my mind as the beauties of nature I found here."

—Daniel Boone speaking of his time exploring Kentucky

CHAPTER

3

SETTLING IN
KENTUCKY

At the end of the French and Indian War (1754–1763), Britain's King George III issued the "Proclamation of 1763." It set aside the lands between the original 13 colonies and the Mississippi River as a hunting ground for American Indians. According to the proclamation, it was against the law to buy the land or to make agreements with the tribes living there. This included Kentucky. The proclamation annoyed colonists, but most simply ignored it.

The First Attempt: Disaster

Boone ignored the proclamation and the fact that American Indians controlled the land. He began leading his family to Kentucky on September 25, 1773. His wife's family and five others accompanied them. The trail was too narrow for wagons, so they walked single-file, climbing over dead brush and pushing aside tall weeds. They climbed steep mountains and waded across streams. They took only what they could carry or pack onto horses. Hogs and cattle followed behind.

In 1773 it was against the law to settle in Kentucky. But that didn't stop Daniel Boone and about 50 others from trying to move there.

When they reached the Powell River Valley, Boone sent his 16-year-old son, James, to Castle's Woods (now Castlewood, Virginia). Cousins John and Richard Mendenhall accompanied him. There they met Captain William Russell and several other men who planned to join Boone's group. However, Russell told them that he would catch up later. Instead, Russell sent his son and four other men with James and the Mendenhalls.

As white settlers continued to move west, American Indian attacks became more frequent.

On the night of October 9, James Boone's group camped beside Wallen's Creek. Fearing that the white settlers had come to take over their land, Shawnee warriors attacked the camp at dawn. James Boone and five others were tortured and killed. Three others escaped. Overcome by the loss, Daniel Boone and his family remained near Castle's Woods for the next two years. Many others in their party returned to North Carolina.

War

News of the attack spread quickly and led to increased conflicts between settlers and the Shawnee. The conflict that followed was known as Lord Dunmore's War (1774), named for Virginia's governor.

During Lord Dunmore's War, Boone served as a captain in the **militia**. He and his troops helped protect travelers from attack. When Lord Dunmore announced plans to invade Shawnee settlements, Shawnee chief Cornstalk agreed to a peace treaty. The fighting stopped—at least for a while.

Transylvania

Several land **speculators** took advantage of the peace treaty. Among them were Judge Richard Henderson and his wealthy partners, who formed the Transylvania Company. Henderson convinced several Cherokee chiefs to sell him 20 million acres (8.1 million hectares) of land (parts of present-day Kentucky and Tennessee). Henderson named the area Transylvania and claimed it would be America's 14th colony.

Henderson hired Boone to cut a road through the wilderness. Widening the existing path would make the settlement of Kentucky and Tennessee easier. The Wilderness Road would also allow more people to travel farther west across the Appalachian Mountains. Henderson promised Boone 2,000 acres (809 hectares) of land in Kentucky for his efforts.

The Wilderness Road

Boone and his crew were to mark a trail so that travelers on foot or on horseback could reach Kentucky. Blazing a trail through the mountains to Kentucky was no easy task, so Boone chose his crew carefully. All the men were woodsmen who were equally skilled with an ax or a rifle. They would need both. Axes were used to cut through the trees and underbrush. Rifles were needed for protection from whatever might be lurking in the forests. In exchange for their hard work, the crew would earn some money and the chance to claim land in Kentucky.

THE WILDERNESS ROAD

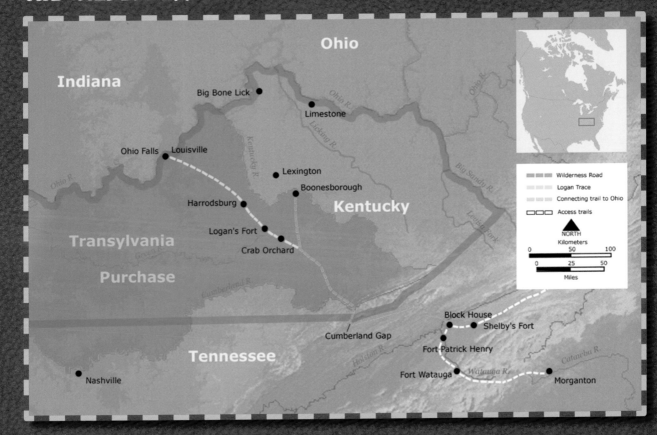

Ohio

Indiana

Big Bone Lick

Limestone

Ohio R.

Ohio Falls Louisville

Kentucky R.

Licking R.

Big Sandy R.

Lexington

Boonesborough

Harrodsburg

Kentucky

Levisa Fork

Logan's Fort

Transylvania

Crab Orchard

Goose

Purchase

Cumberland R.

Block House

Shelby's Fort

Fort Patrick Henry

Catawba R.

Cumberland Gap

Tennessee

Fort Watauga

Watauga R.

Morganton

Holston R.

Nashville

Legend
- Wilderness Road
- Logan Trace
- Connecting trail to Ohio
- Access trails

NORTH

Kilometers
0   50   100

0   25   50
Miles

Boone and his crew began their journey on March 10, 1775. The Wilderness Road followed the Warrior's Path and trails worn down by migrating buffalo. Boone led the way at the head of the pack. Whenever possible, he chose shallow river crossings and open spaces between the mountains similar to the Cumberland Gap. The men followed with their axes swinging. They cleared away brush and downed trees, moved large rocks out of the way, and placed logs over swamps and creeks. They chopped down trees and briar bushes, pulled stubborn roots out of the ground, and hacked through patches of cane. They worked in snow and freezing rain. They splashed through rivers and squished through mud. Their arms ached and their hands stiffened after hours of backbreaking work.

For nearly 200 miles (322 km), Boone and his crew hacked away trees and bushes to blaze the trail known as the Wilderness Road.

Wolves howled, wildcats screamed, and bears prowled. Copperheads and rattlesnakes slithered nearby. But the greatest fear was of Native American attacks. During the first two weeks, they did not see a single warrior. But their luck would not last.

Surprise Attack!

On the night of March 24, Boone and his crew camped at Silver Creek, just 15 miles (24 km) from their final destination. Just before dawn the next day, war whoops woke them as Indians **ambushed** the camp swinging tomahawks and shooting rifles. They vanished as suddenly as they had appeared, but not before killing two of Boone's men and wounding another.

Finally on April 6, 1775, Boone and his crew reached Big Lick—a level plain on the Kentucky River (near present-day Richmond, Kentucky). They cleared land, built a fort, and planted crops. They named the new settlement Boonesborough.

"He attended me as his child, cured my wounds by the use of medicines from the woods, and nursed me with paternal affection until I recovered."

—Felix Walker, recalling how Daniel Boone cared for him after he was wounded at Silver Creek

CHAPTER

4

THE FAR SIDE OF THE REVOLUTION

The first shots of the Revolutionary War (1775–1783) were fired shortly after Boone and his crew completed the Wilderness Road. The major battles of the war were fought far from Kentucky, but the British did not ignore the settlements there. The British provided guns to the Cherokee and Shawnee, who were eager to stop the takeover of their hunting grounds. American Indian raids on Kentucky settlements were frequent and violent.

The Boones Try Again

In August 1775 Boone led his family and several others through the Cumberland Gap. This time the Boones made it to Boonesborough and settled there. About half of the others continued west to Harrodsburg, about 50 miles (80 km) away.

Troubling Times

By the spring of 1776, only 200 of Kentucky's first 500 pioneers remained there. All of the earliest towns faced Indian attacks and kidnappings. The settlers lived within the forts and kept loaded rifles close by in case of attack.

The settlers also lacked medical care and were always short of supplies. Farming was nearly impossible because the fields were outside the protection of the fort. Even going to the rivers to fish or fetch water was dangerous.

KIDNAPPING JEMIMA

On July 14, 1776, Daniel Boone's 13-year-old daughter, Jemima, and two friends were kidnapped by five American Indians. Residents of Boonesborough heard the girls screaming and Daniel Boone and other men quickly organized a rescue party.

After three days of scouting through the wilderness, Boone and his men finally caught up to the girls and their kidnappers. Boone's men shot at the Indians who fled in fear. The girls were safe, but the kidnapping increased the hatred between white settlers and Native Americans. Many settlers left Kentucky as a result.

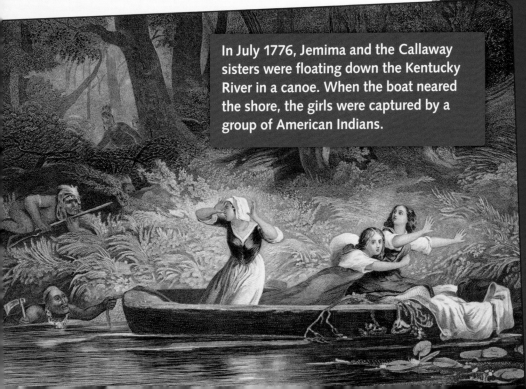

In July 1776, Jemima and the Callaway sisters were floating down the Kentucky River in a canoe. When the boat neared the shore, the girls were captured by a group of American Indians.

Captured!

On January 8, 1778, Daniel Boone and 30 men from Boonesborough left for Blue Licks to get salt to preserve meat. But four Shawnee braves captured Boone on February 7. While at the Shawnee camp, Boone learned that Chief Blackfish planned to attack Boonesborough and take its residents captive. Boone knew that the women and children could not survive a 10-day march to the Shawnee village during the winter. He promised Blackfish that his men at the salt lick would surrender if the chief would delay the attack until spring.

Blackfish agreed, and Boone's men surrendered. Many of them were adopted by the Shawnee, as was the custom. Blackfish, who had recently lost a son, adopted Boone. He called him "Shel-tow-ee" or "Big Turtle."

> "I became a son, and had a great share in the affection of my new parents, brothers, sisters, and friends. I was exceedingly familiar and friendly with them, always appearing as chearful and satisfied as possible, and they put great confidence in me."

—Daniel Boone speaking of his adoption by the Shawnee

Escape

Boone remained with the Shawnee for five months, waiting for a chance to escape. One day while hunting with several warriors, Boone stole a pony and escaped. When he arrived in Boonesborough, he rallied the men to finish work on the fort and prepare for battle.

The Battle for Boonesborough

Although greatly outnumbered, the residents of Boonesborough defended their fort against a group of Shawnee warriors.

On September 7, 1778, 50 to 60 residents of Boonesborough faced off against more than 400 Shawnee warriors. Boone tried to convince Blackfish to leave in peace. He also hoped talking to the Shawnee chief would delay fighting until help arrived. But help never came.

The Shawnee warriors tried to burn the fort and build a tunnel into it. But Boone came up with one plan after another to save the fort. Finally, after nine days, the Shawnee gave up.

When Boone had arrived in Boonesborough, he learned that Rebecca and the children had returned to North Carolina. So after the attack, he returned to his family in North Carolina. But he couldn't stay away from Kentucky for long. In the fall of 1779, he led his family and a new group of settlers to Kentucky. However, by this time Boonesborough was growing rapidly, and Boone soon felt that the town was too crowded. He moved his family a few miles north to another town that took his name, Boone's Station.

Thousands Take the Wilderness Road

After America declared its independence in 1776, the Proclamation of 1763 was no longer in force. Anyone could settle in Kentucky. So by 1781 as the Revolutionary War was winding down, many soldiers were granted land in Kentucky in return for their service. Farmers were attracted by offers of cheap land, space to expand, and the opportunity to make a fresh start.

The Wilderness Road played an important role in the westward expansion of the United States.

But traveling the Wilderness Road took two to three weeks in the best conditions. Many families were so poor that they were forced to make the

journey without shoes or socks, even in ice and snow. Some turned back, but thousands crossed the Cumberland Gap into Kentucky in the late 1700s.

These pioneers climbed up and down steep mountains. Many times when the trail was snowy or muddy, livestock, tools, and supplies slid down mountainsides or fell over cliffs. Many drowned while crossing swift-flowing waterways. Others were killed by Indians. Some ran out of food and dry clothes and suffered illnesses such as **measles** and **smallpox**. Howling wolves and bears also frightened them.

Despite the dangers, nearly 300,000 settlers traveled the Wilderness Road between 1775 and 1800. As a result, Kentucky's population grew from about 200 in 1776 to 221,000 in 1800. Some adventurers even continued past the Mississippi River, America's western border at the time.

CHAPTER 5

DANIEL BOONE: LOOKING BACK

Daniel Boone never received the land that Richard Henderson had promised him in exchange for cutting the Wilderness Road. Other people claimed the same lands as Boone, which was common at the time. Often the same land was sold twice or boundaries were unclear. Boone made several land claims over the years but lost them in court battles.

New Roads to Kentucky

In 1792 Kentucky became the 15th state. Between 1795 and 1796 the Kentucky portion of the Wilderness Road was widened for wagons crossing the Cumberland Gap.

After the Erie Canal was completed in 1825, large riverboats carried passengers down the Ohio River and west on the Missouri. When the National Road opened in 1834, many settlers used it to travel from Cumberland, Maryland, to the Ohio River. By 1840 few travelers used the original Wilderness Road to reach Kentucky.

After 1825, when the Erie Canal was completed, traffic on the Wilderness Road slowed down.

DANIEL BOONE'S "AUTOBIOGRAPHY"

In 1784 pioneer John Filson published *The Discovery, Settlement, and Present State of Kentucke*. The book gave a glowing review of Kentucky and included a map that led thousands of settlers to the area.

At the end of the book, Filson added a section called "The Adventures of Col. Daniel Boon." Filson referred to it as Daniel Boone's **autobiography**. However, the author probably wrote the text himself based on stories Boone had told him. Either way, Filson's book made Daniel Boone famous. But this sudden fame didn't change the **frontiersman**. He continued to hunt and explore the wilderness.

An American Hero

Daniel Boone left Kentucky in 1799. When asked why, he said, "Too crowded ... I want more elbow-room." When Boone was offered free land in exchange for leading a group of pioneers to Missouri, he moved his family about 60 miles (97 km) west of St. Louis.

Daniel Boone never lost his passion for exploring. He took his last long hunt in 1817 at age 82. He died in 1820, at age 85. He was a trailblazer who sparked a land boom in Kentucky. His efforts also paved the way for those wanting to explore the lands west of the Appalachian Mountains.

TIMELINE

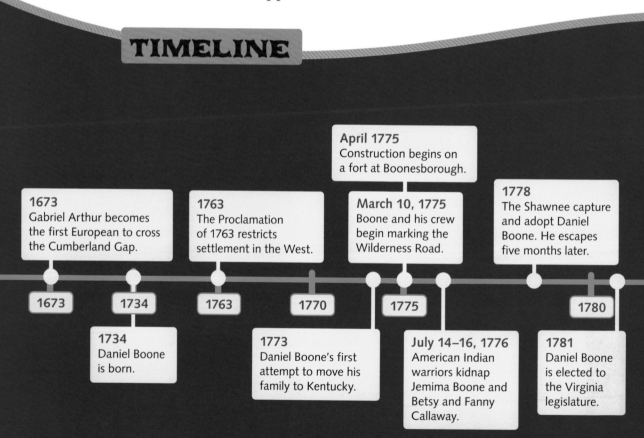

1673
Gabriel Arthur becomes the first European to cross the Cumberland Gap.

1763
The Proclamation of 1763 restricts settlement in the West.

April 1775
Construction begins on a fort at Boonesborough.

March 10, 1775
Boone and his crew begin marking the Wilderness Road.

1778
The Shawnee capture and adopt Daniel Boone. He escapes five months later.

1673   1734   1763   1770   1775   1780

1734
Daniel Boone is born.

1773
Daniel Boone's first attempt to move his family to Kentucky.

July 14–16, 1776
American Indian warriors kidnap Jemima Boone and Betsy and Fanny Callaway.

1781
Daniel Boone is elected to the Virginia legislature.

CUMBERLAND GAP NATIONAL HISTORICAL PARK

Today the National Park Service maintains the Cumberland Gap National Historical Park. The entrance to the park is in Middleboro, Kentucky, but the park includes parts of Kentucky, Tennessee, and Virginia. More than 700,000 people visit the park each year. Adventurous types can hike along a 2-mile- (3.2-km) stretch of the original Wilderness Road.

In 1996 the mile-long Cumberland Gap Tunnel opened where the states of Kentucky, Tennessee, and Virginia meet. Each year about 11 million cars pass through the tunnel.

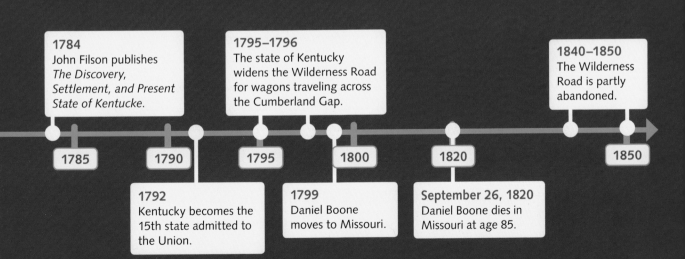

1784
John Filson publishes *The Discovery, Settlement, and Present State of Kentucke.*

1785

1792
Kentucky becomes the 15th state admitted to the Union.

1790

1795–1796
The state of Kentucky widens the Wilderness Road for wagons traveling across the Cumberland Gap.

1795

1799
Daniel Boone moves to Missouri.

1800

September 26, 1820
Daniel Boone dies in Missouri at age 85.

1820

1840–1850
The Wilderness Road is partly abandoned.

1850

GLOSSARY

ambush (AM-bush)—a surprise attack

autobiography (aw-tuh-by-AH-gruh-fee)—the story of a person's own life written by that person

barter (BAR-tur)—to trade food or goods and services instead of using money

cane (KAYN)—a plant with a long, hollow or jointed woody stem that can grow to more than 15 feet (4.6 meters) tall

destination (des-tuh-NAY-shuh)—the place to which one is traveling

frontiersman (fruhn-TIHRZ-muhn)—a person who is skilled at living on unsettled land

game (GAME)—wild mammals and birds that are hunted for sport or food

indentured servant (in-DEN-churd SERV-uhnt)—a person who works for someone else for a period of time in return for payment of travel and living costs

marksman (MARKS-muhn)—a person skilled at aiming and shooting guns

measles (MEE-zuhlz)—an infectious disease causing a fever and a rash

militia (muh-LISH-uh)—a group of volunteer citizens who are organized to fight but are not professional soldiers

smallpox (SMAWL-poks)—a disease that spreads easily from person to person, causing chills, fever, and pimples

speculator (SPEK-yuh-ley-ter)—a person who buy goods or property with the expectation of selling at a higher price in the future

READ MORE

Adler, David A. and Michael S. Adler. *A Picture Book of Daniel Boone.* Picture Book Biographies. New York: Holiday House, 2013.

Kennedy, Emily. *Daniel Boone and His Adventures.* American Legends and Folktales. New York: Cavendish Square Publishing, 2014.

McCarthy, Pat. *Daniel Boone: American Pioneer and Frontiersman.* Legendary American Biographies. Berkeley Heights, N.J.: Enslow Publishers, Inc., 2015.

Sanford, William R. and Carl R. Green. *Daniel Boone: Courageous Frontiersman.* Courageous Heroes of the American West. Berkeley Heights, N.J.: Enslow Publishers, Inc., 2013.

INTERNET SITES

FactHound offers a safe, fun way to find Internet sites related to this book. All of the sites on FactHound have been researched by our staff.

Here's all you do:

Visit *www.facthound.com*

Type in this code: 9781491448953

Super-cool stuff!

Check out projects, games and lots more at
www.capstonekids.com

CRITICAL THINKING USING THE COMMON CORE

1. If Daniel Boone had never returned to Kentucky after his son James was killed, how do you think the settlement of Kentucky may have changed? (Integration of Knowledge and Ideas)

2. Using details from the text, describe how the Cumberland Gap affected the settlement of Kentucky. (Key Ideas and Details)

3. Daniel Boone moved whenever a town became too crowded. How do you think he would feel about living in today's society? Where would he live? (Text Types and Purposes)

INDEX